AL LEONARD

DRUMSET FILLS
500 FILLS • ALL STYLES • ALL LEVELS

BY JOHN CALARCO

Edited by Rick Mattingly

To access audio visit:
www.halleonard.com/mylibrary

Enter Code
7136-3936-5491-1784

ISBN 978-1-4803-9972-3

HAL•LEONARD®
CORPORATION

7777 W. BLUEMOUND RD. P.O. BOX 13819 MILWAUKEE, WI 53213

In Australia Contact:
Hal Leonard Australia Pty. Ltd.
4 Lentara Court
Cheltenham, Victoria, 3192 Australia
Email: ausadmin@halleonard.com.au

Visit Hal Leonard Online at
www.halleonard.com

NOTATION LEGEND

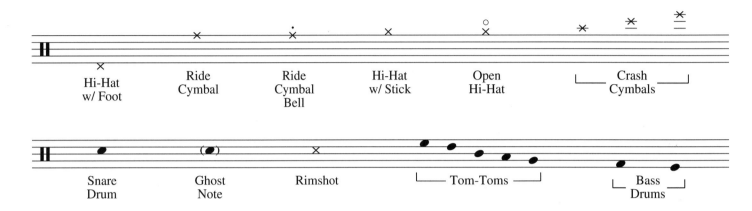

TABLE OF CONTENTS

INTRODUCTION

Hello Drummer Enthusiasts!

I've organized the drum fills in this book into genres where they would most likely be played. Many of the fills are not exclusive to any one style, but for the sake of organization, they are categorized to give you a starting point. I encourage you to apply the fills to other genres and interpret them in your own way. In many ways, this is a book of ideas that I hope will inspire you to forge your own style.

You will also notice that some drum fills come with certain sticking patterns. Again, this is just a starting point to help those who may not know where to start. I have purposely left out most sticking combinations in the hope that the student will come up with their own.

It's within these little discoveries that what I term "happy accidents" sometimes occur. These little "happy accidents" are what can lead to something entirely new, and that is my intent for every student looking over these fills. In short, I hope you eventually make all these fills your own!

My main hope is that you have as much fun applying these fills as I had putting this book together! If this book can help those who may be "stuck" overcome any obstacles they might have, then my efforts will have been successful. Peace and God bless.

Johnny "Cee" Calarco

I'd like to thank Jeff Schroedl for asking me to do this. Also, Jackie Muth for her keen eyes and ears as well as consummate professionalism, all the musicians I've been blessed to play with over the years, and our Divine Creator who makes it all possible. Peace!

ABOUT THE AUTHOR

John Calarco's (aka Johnny Cee) obsession with rhythm started at the tender age of five with him pounding on Jay's Potato Chip® cartons using forks and spoons. That began his drumming journey, playing to an eclectic mix of many musical styles steadily supplied by his mother and older brother from the Beatles to Zep to Miles Davis and everything in between. His first professional gig at the age of eleven was in a big band. Soon thereafter, jazz/fusion and rock 'n' roll ruled his life.

By age seventeen he began playing the local music scene around Chicago and Milwaukee, immediately garnering a reputation as a "monster" player. By nineteen, he had established himself solidly in the music scene through a Milwaukee band that almost literally blew up overnight. Big Bang Theory, almost instantly, became a wildly popular funk band opening for the likes of James Brown and other national artists of that level. A world tour in 1996 with Willy Porter (where Willy and band opened for and performed with Tori Amos) really set the tone for good things to come, ultimately leading to a move for young John Cee to New York City and his introduction to a multitude of artists and musicians.

While there, John was invited to play with NYC's famed Blue Man Group, supplying income and proximity to even more artists such as Joy Askew (Peter Gabriel), Oskar Kartya (Spiro Gyra), Tony Jarvis (EMI artist), and many others. Returning home in 2001, John began playing and touring with Fender Musical Instruments' top clinician, Greg Koch, who took him all over the world and allowed him to perform with many more world-renown artists and musicians.

During 2002, John, also a songwriter and lead singer, fronted and played alongside fellow drummer Todd Sucherman (Styx) in the popular band, NC-17. During this period, John and Todd became close friends, sharing the stage several times with the classic progressive rock of early Genesis material. This led to a six-year partnership with Genesis/Phil Collins' guitarist Daryl Stuermer, during which John recorded several CDs with Stuermer. A list of some of the people John has toured/recorded or performed with includes Roscoe Beck (bassist for Leonard Cohen), Reggie Hamilton (bassist for Seal), The Brothers Johnson, Freedy Johnston, Mike Keneally (Frank Zappa), Bob Lizik (bassist for Brian Wilson), Nils Lofgren (Bruce Springsteen), Kate Pierson (B52s), Andy Summers (The Police), and many more.

Johnny Cee has also released his first solo CD, *Shine*, which features his vocals and songwriting. An instrumental CD featuring John's drumming is soon to follow!

For more information please visit John's website at www.johnny-cee-calarco.com

ROCK

SIMPLE ROCK FILLS

1.

2.

3.

4.

5.
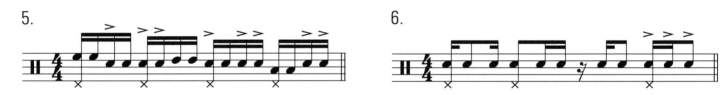

6.
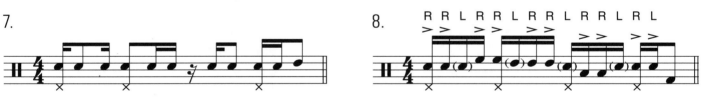

7.

8.

9.

10.

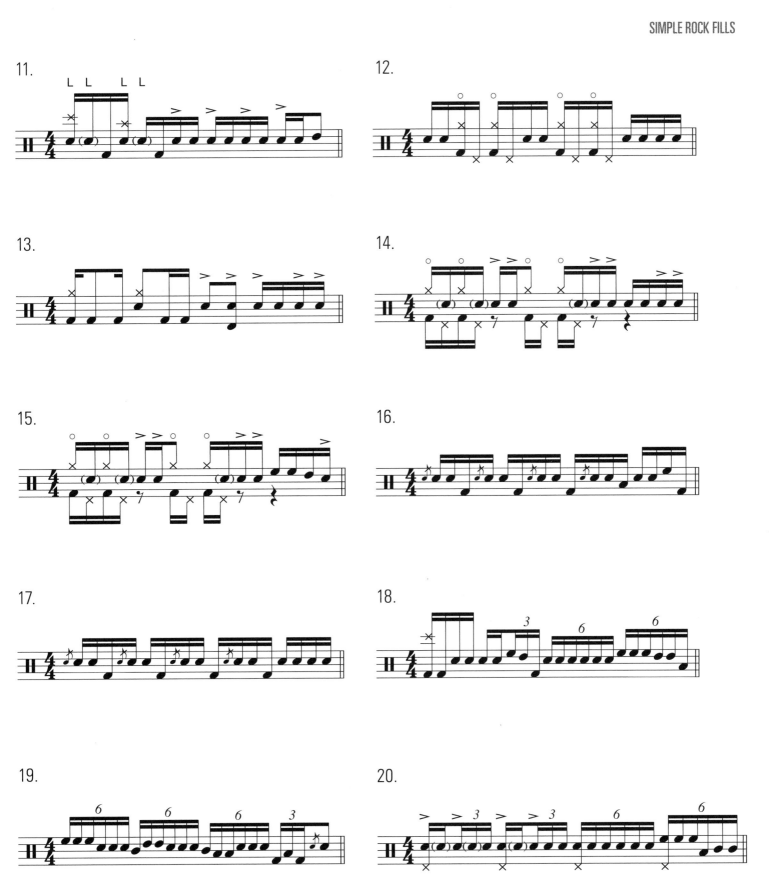

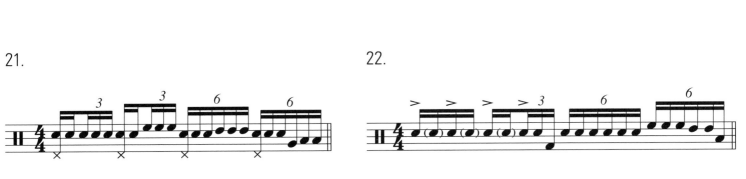

23.

24.

RF LF RF

25.

26.

RF LF RF LF RF   RF

27.

28.

29.

30.

31.

32.

SIMPLE 2/4 ROCK FILLS

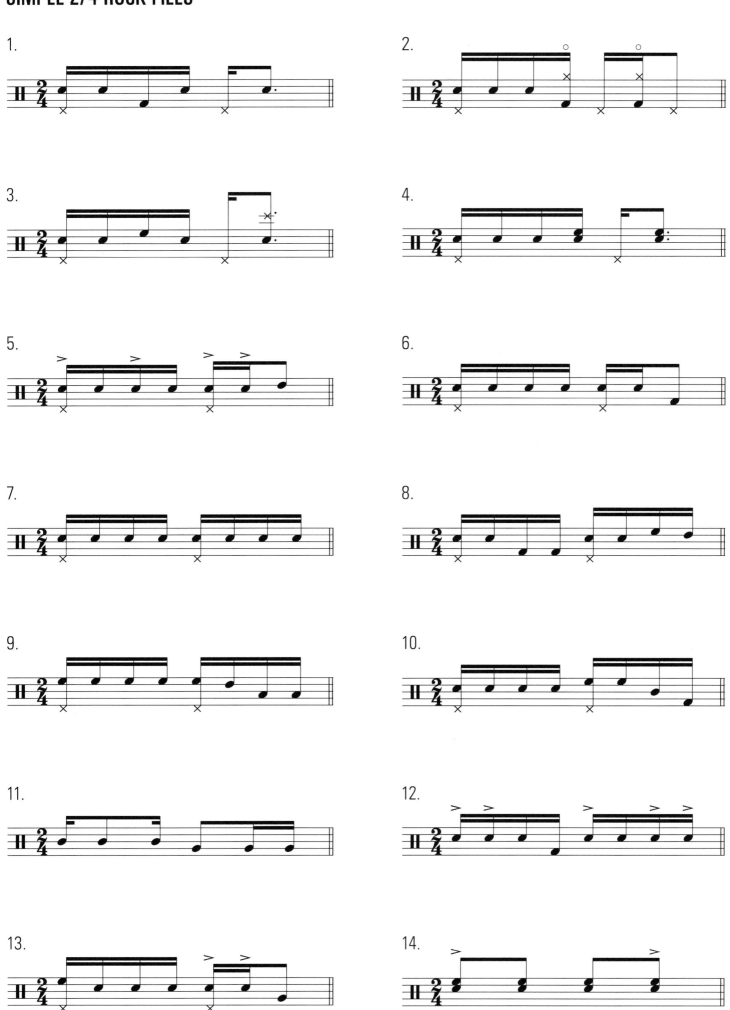

15.

16.

17.

18.

19.

20.

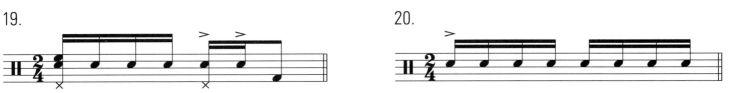

21.

22.

23.

24.

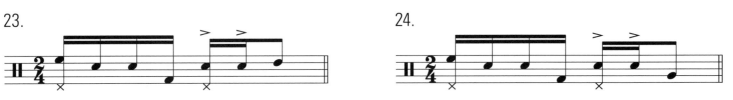

25.

26.

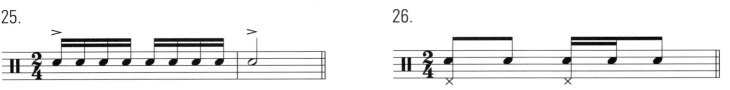

27.

28.

29.

30.

31.

R L R

32.

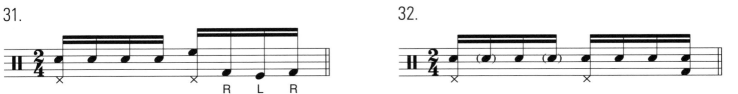

33.

34.

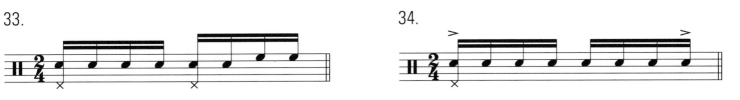

35.

36.

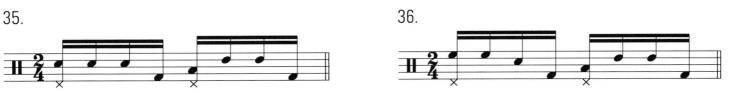

37.

38.

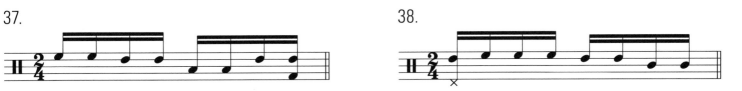

2/4 HEAVY ROCK FILLS

1.
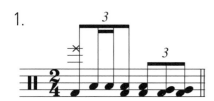

2.

3.
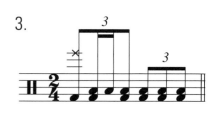

4.
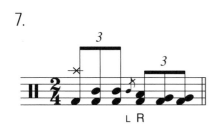

5.

6.

7.

8.

9.

10.

11.

12.
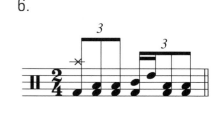

13.
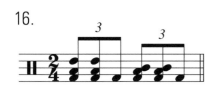

14.

15.

16.
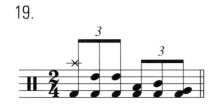

17.

18.

19.
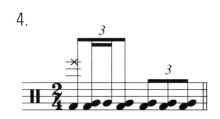

20.
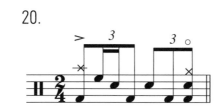

21 .
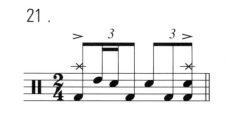

22.
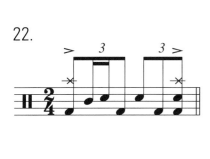

23.
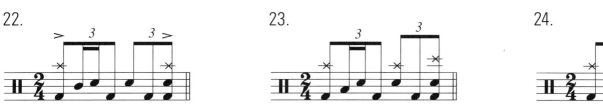

24.
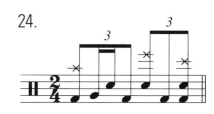

25.

26.
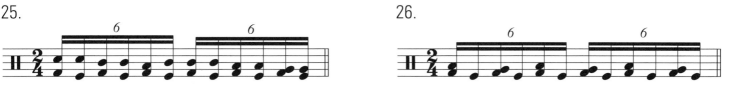

27.
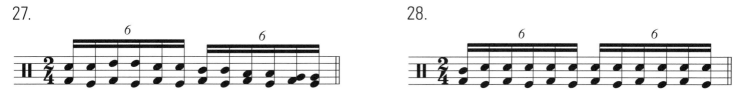

28.

29.

30.
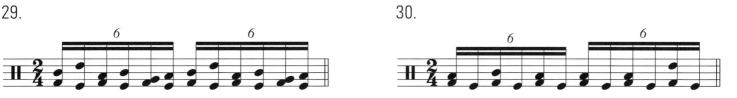

31.

32.
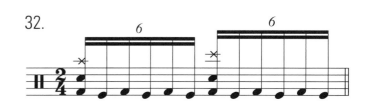

33.

34.

35.
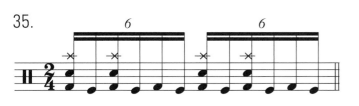

36.
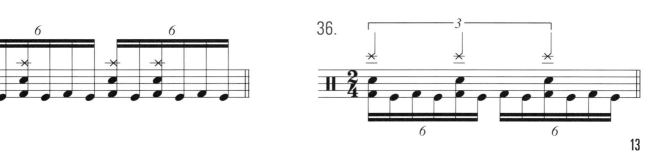

37.

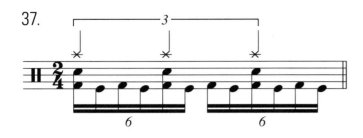

38.

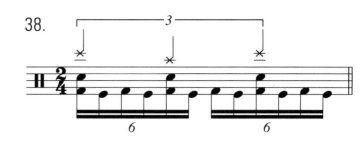

39.

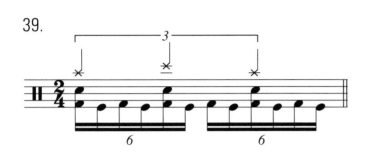

40.

41.

42.

43.

44.

45.

46.

47.

48.

49.

50.

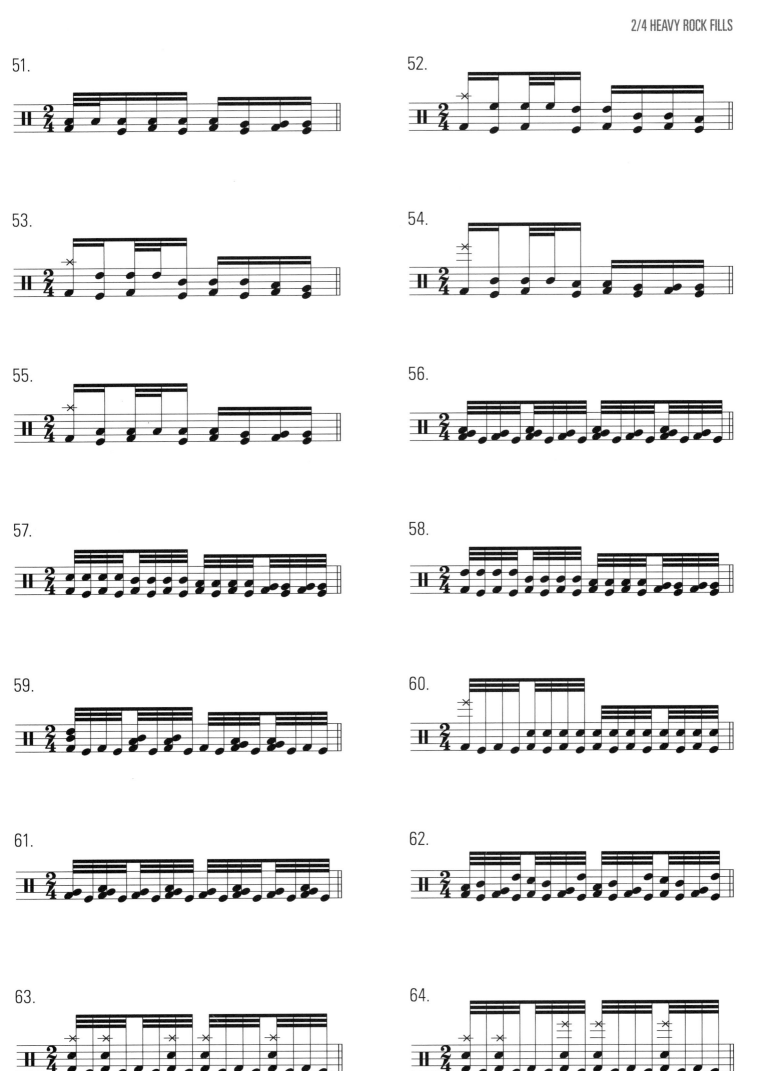

65.

66.

67.

68.

ONE-BEAT HEAVY ROCK FILLS

1.

2.

3.

4.

5.

6.

7.

8.

9.

10.

11.

12.

13.

14.

15.

16.

BLUES AND GOSPEL

BLUES FILLS

1.

2.
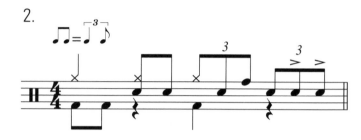

3.

4.

5.

6.
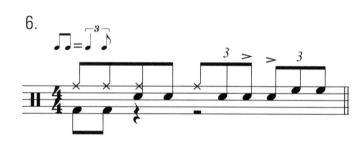

7.

8.
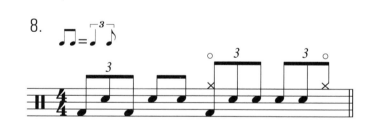

9.

10.

11.

12.

13.

14.

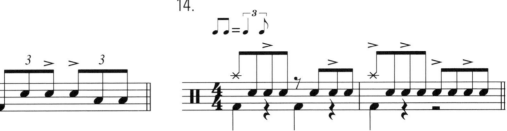

15.

16.

17.

18.

19.

20.

21.

22.

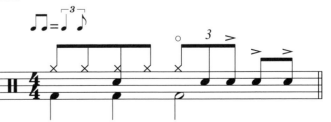

23.

24.

25.
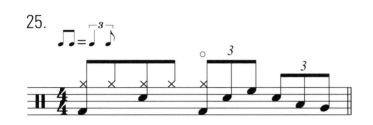

26.

27.
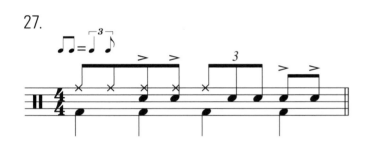

28.
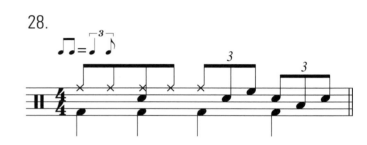

29.
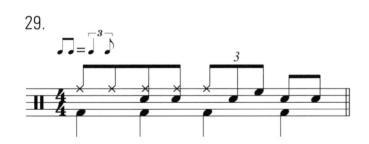

30.
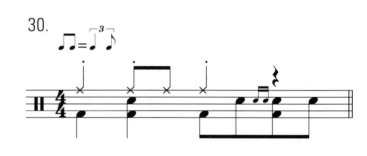

31.
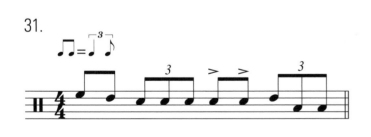

32.
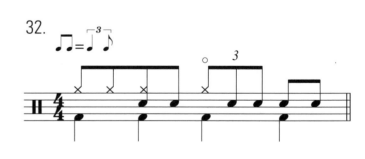

33.
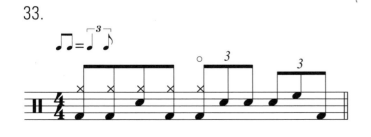

34.

35.
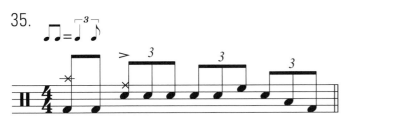

36.
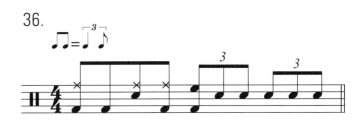

37.

38.

39.

40.
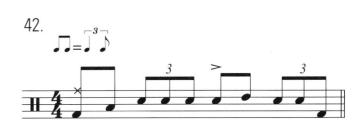

41.
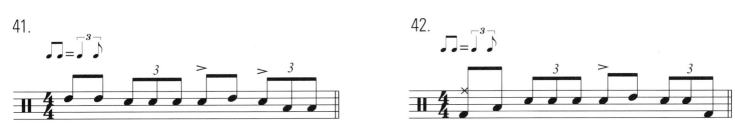

42.
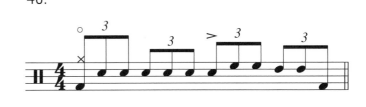

43.
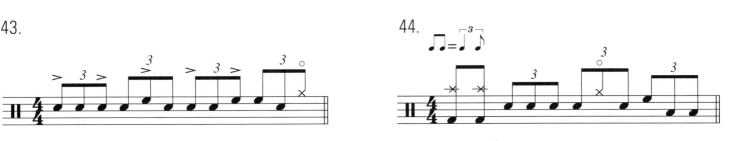

44.
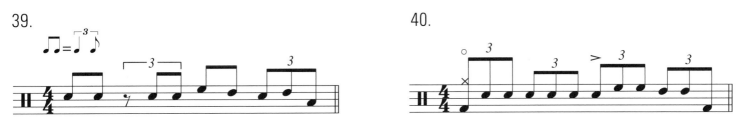

45.
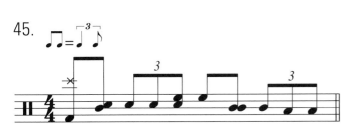

46.
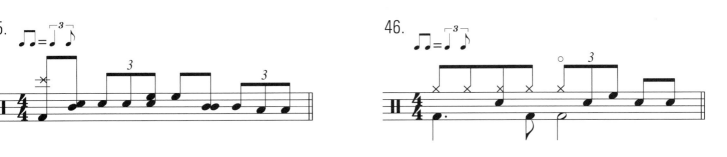

47.
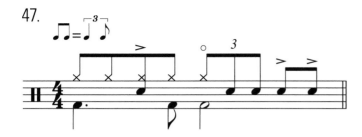

48.
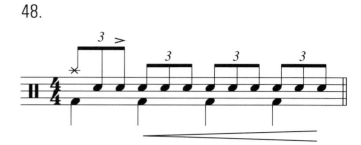

49.

50.
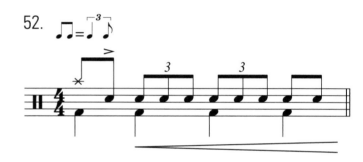

51.
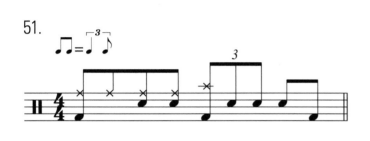

52.
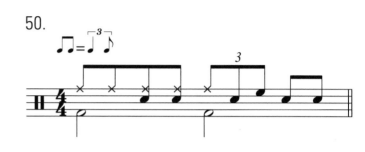

53.
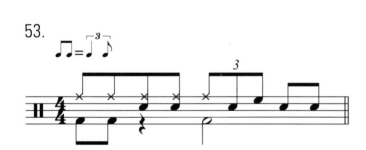

54.
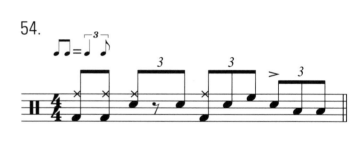

55.
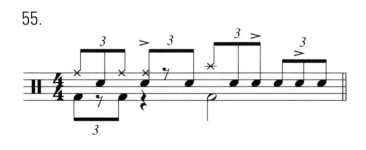

56.
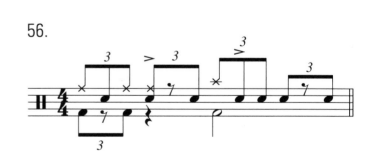

57.
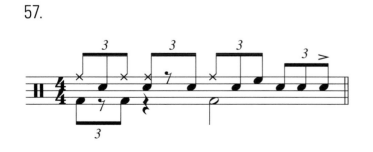

58.
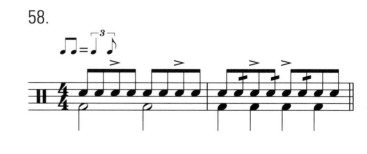

59.

60.
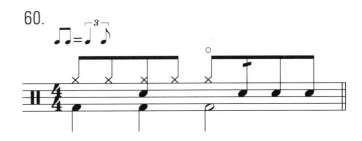

61.
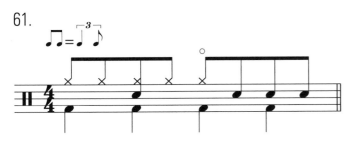

62.
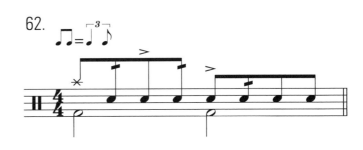

63.
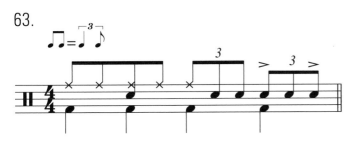

64.
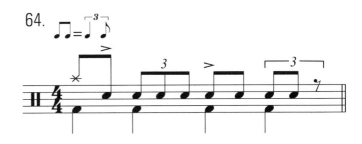

TWO-BEAT GOSPEL FILLS

1.

2.

3.

4.

5.
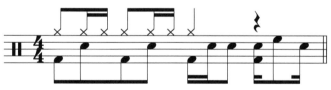

6.

7.

8.

9.

10.

11.

12.
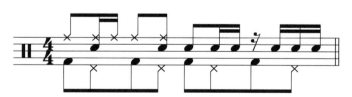

13.
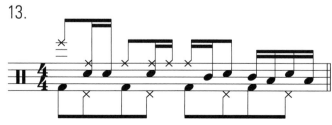

14.
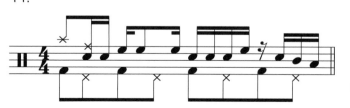

COUNTRY

1.

2.

3.

4.

5.

6.
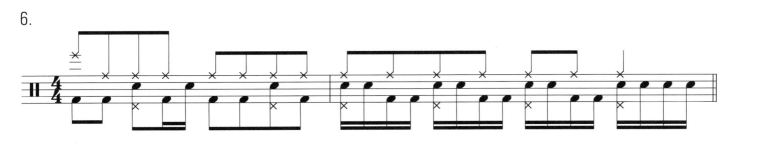

7.

8.

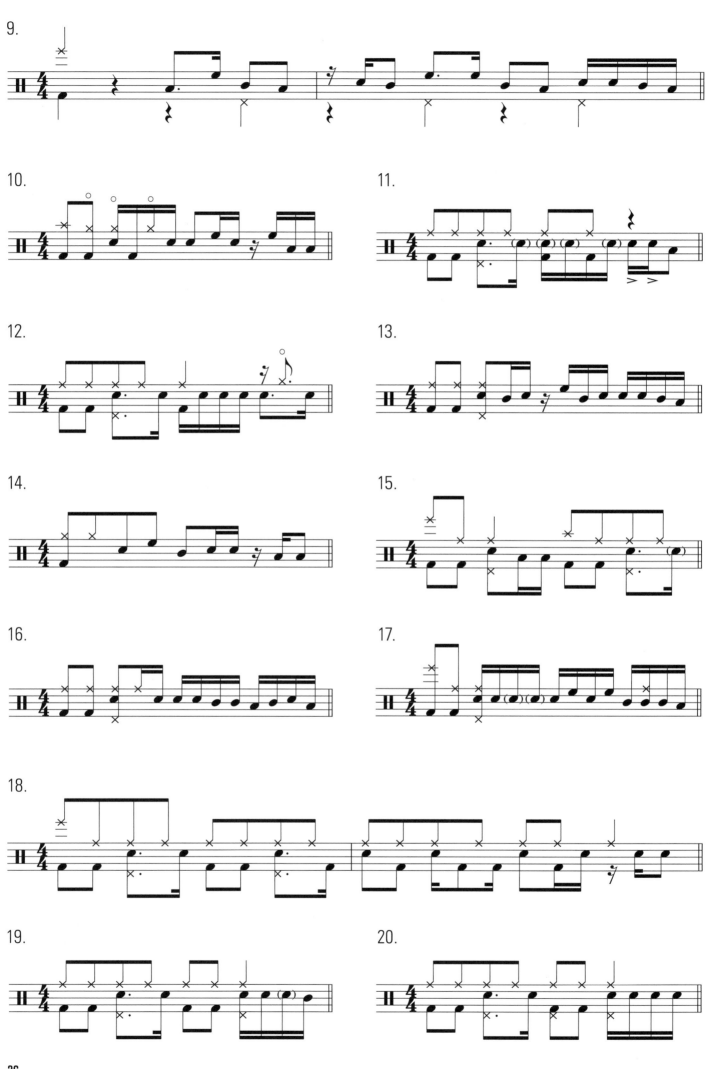

21.

22.

23.

24.

25.

26.

27.

28.

29.

30.
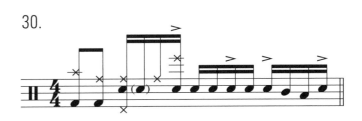

31.

32.
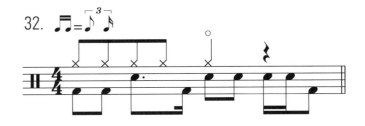

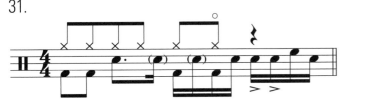

33.

34.

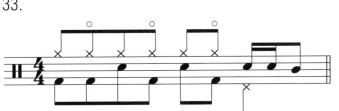

35.

36.

37.

38.

39.

40.
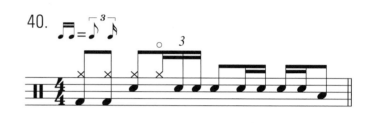

41.

42.

43.

44.
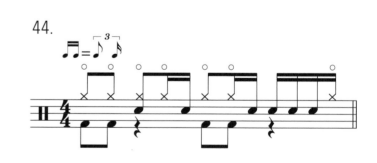

45.

46.
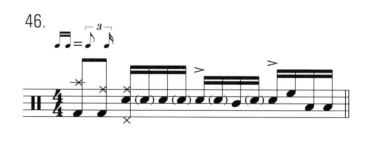

47.

48.

49.

50.
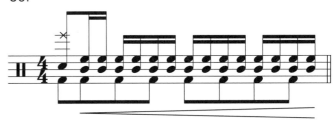

51.

52.

53.

54.

55.

COUNTRY TRAINBEAT FILLS

1.

2.

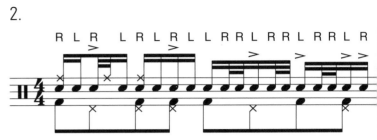

3.

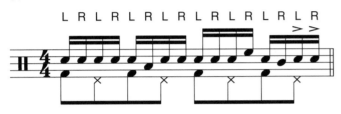

4.

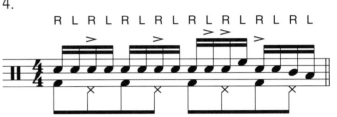

5.

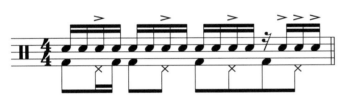

6.

7.

8.

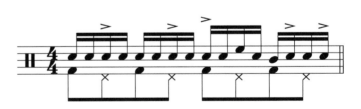

9.

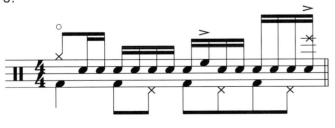

10.

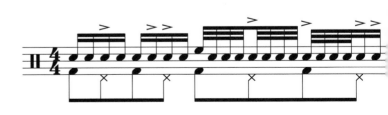

11.

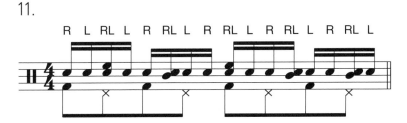

12.

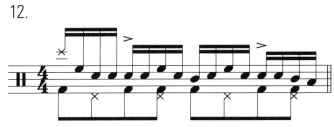

13.

14.

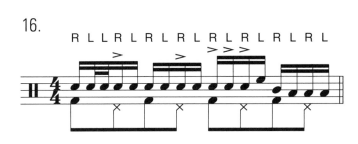

15.

16.

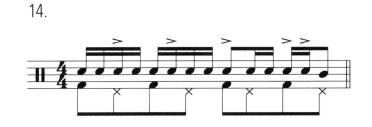

17.

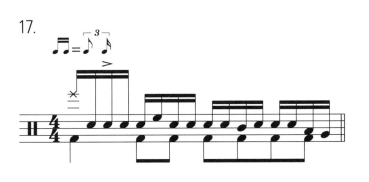

18.

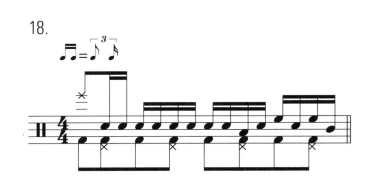

19.

20.

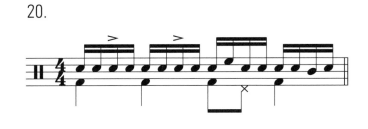

21.

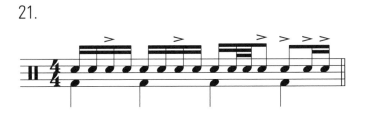

22.

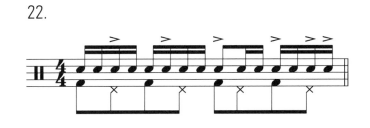

JAZZ, FUSION, AND FUNK

JAZZ FILLS

1.

2.

3.

4.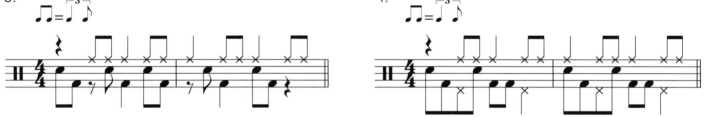

5.

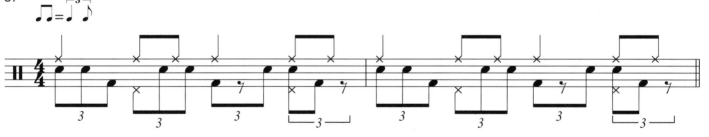

6.

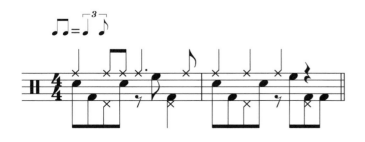

7.

Play hi-hat with foot on 2 and 4 throughout.

8.

9.

Play hi-hat with foot on 2 and 4 throughout.

10.

Play hi-hat with foot on 2 and 4 throughout.

11.

12.

13.

14.

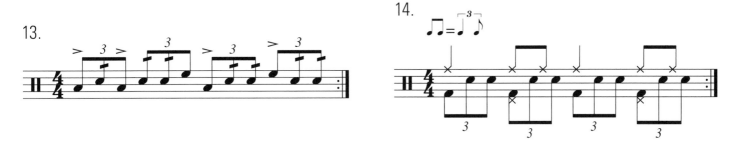

15.

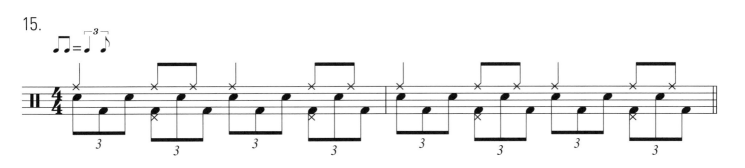

16.

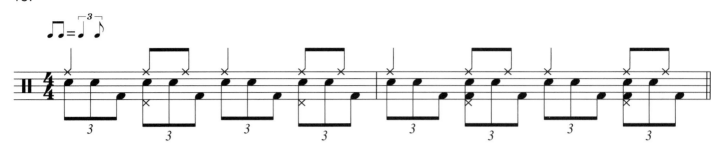

17.

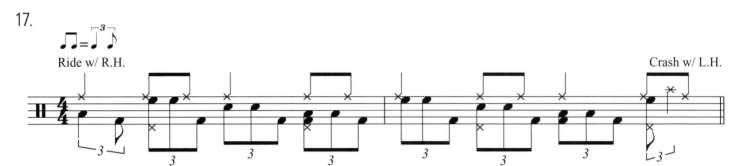

18.

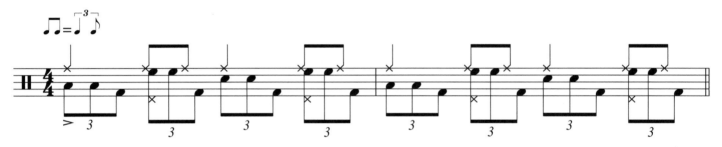

19.

Straight Eighths

20.

Straight Eighths

21.

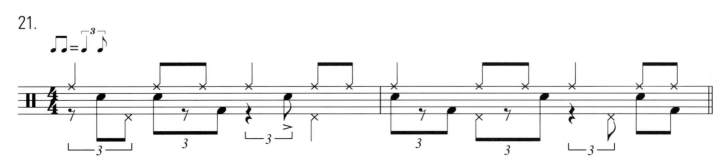

28.

Play hi-hat with foot on 2 and 4.

29.

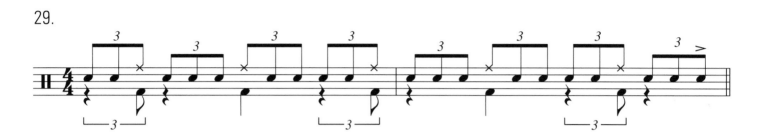

30.

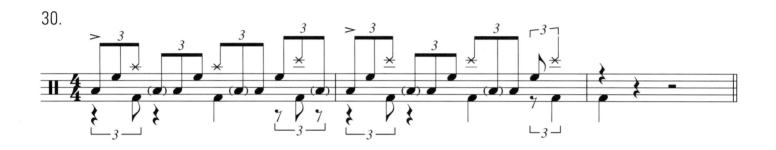

31.

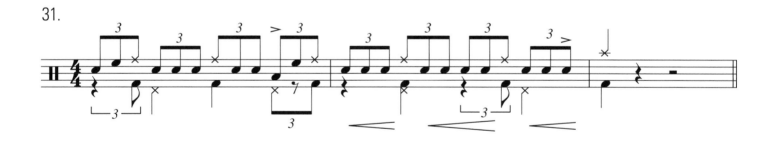

32.

33.

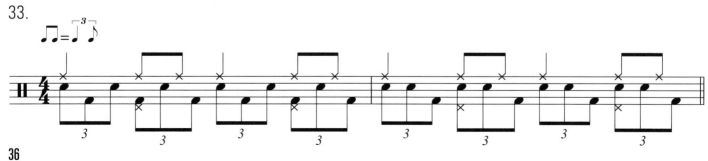

FUSION FILLS

1.

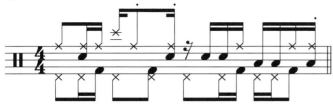

2.

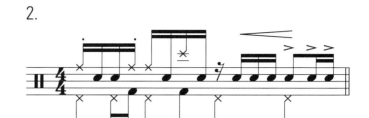

3.

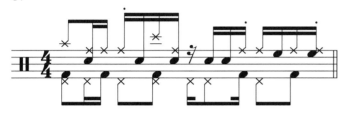

4.

5.

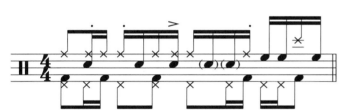

6.

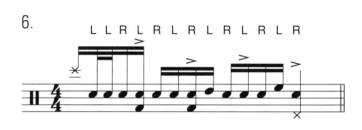

7.

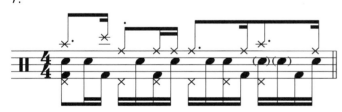

8.

9.

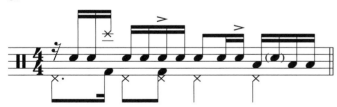

10.

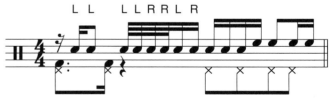

11.

12.

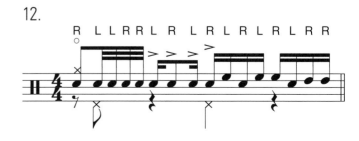

13.

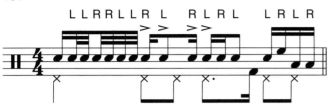

14.

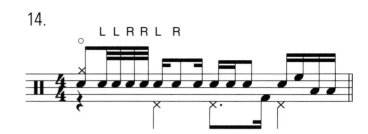

15.

16.

17.

18.

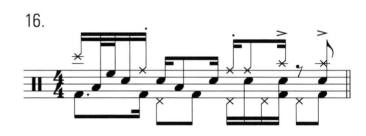

19.

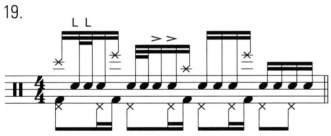

20.

21.

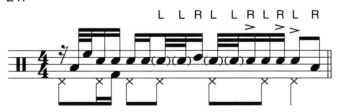

22.

23.

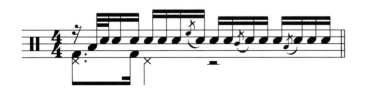

24.

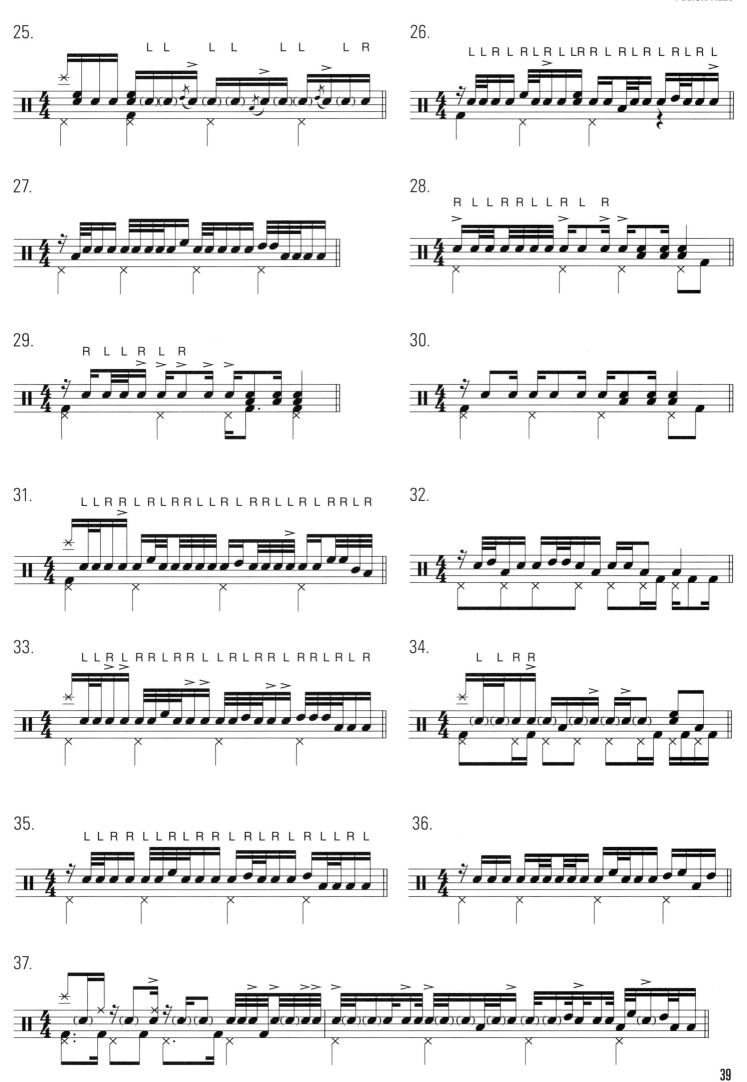

FUNK FILLS

9.

10.

11.

12.

REGGAE AND SKA

REGGAE FILLS

1.
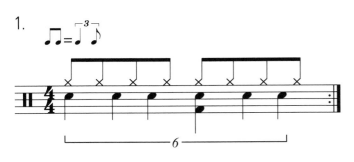

2.

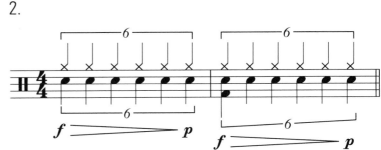

3.
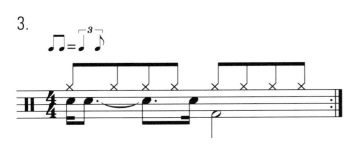

4.

5.
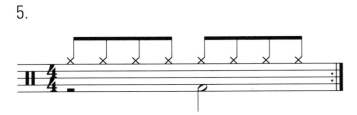

6.

7.
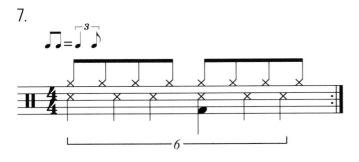

8.

9.
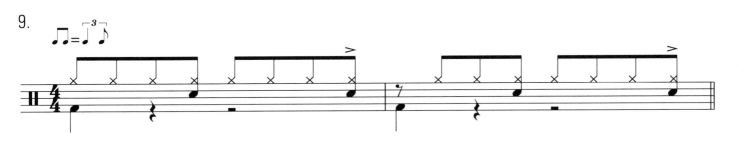

10.

11.

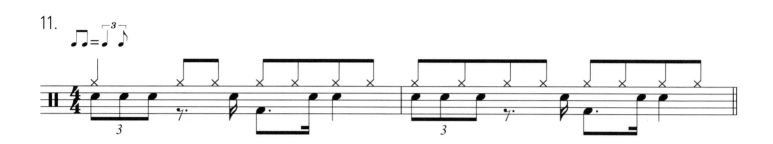

12.

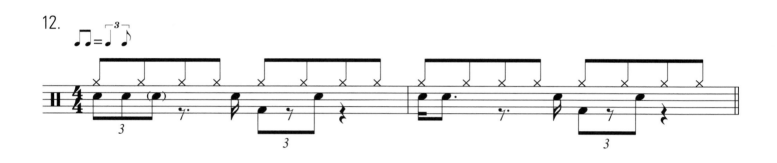

13.

14.

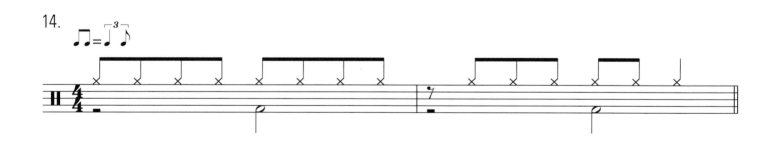

15.

16.

17.

18

19.

20.

Slightly Swing Sixteenths

SKA FILLS

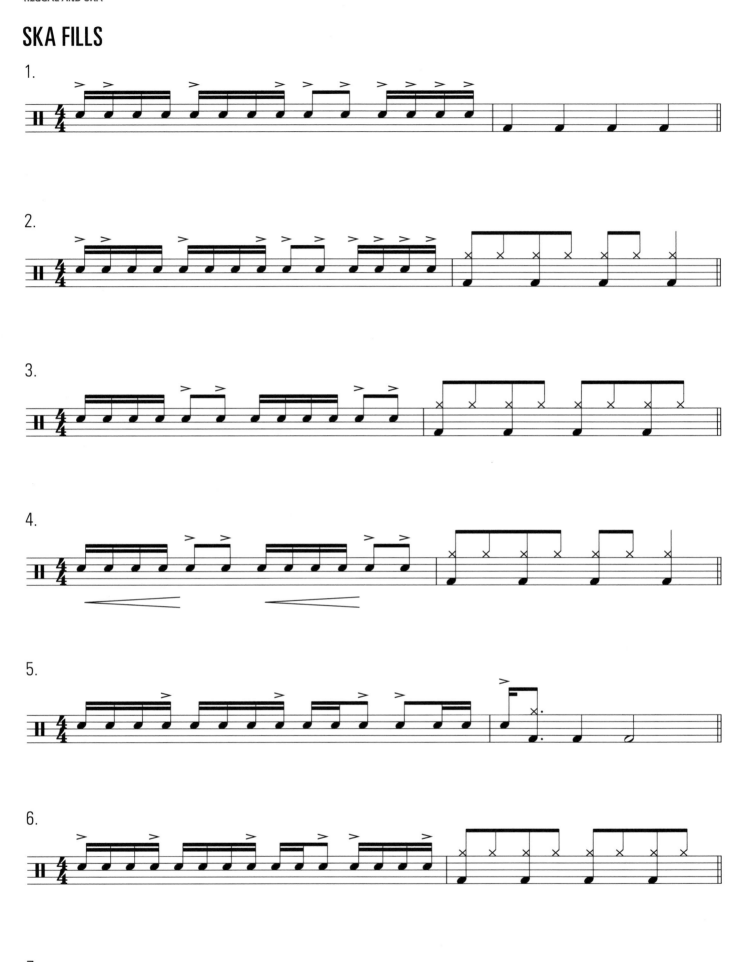

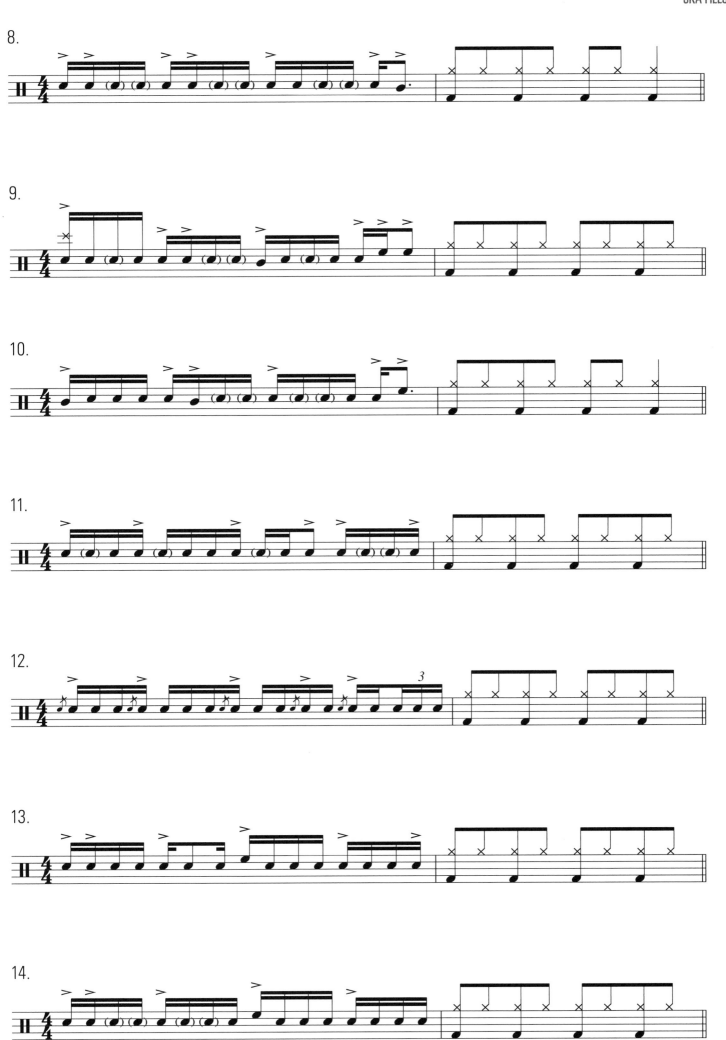

15.

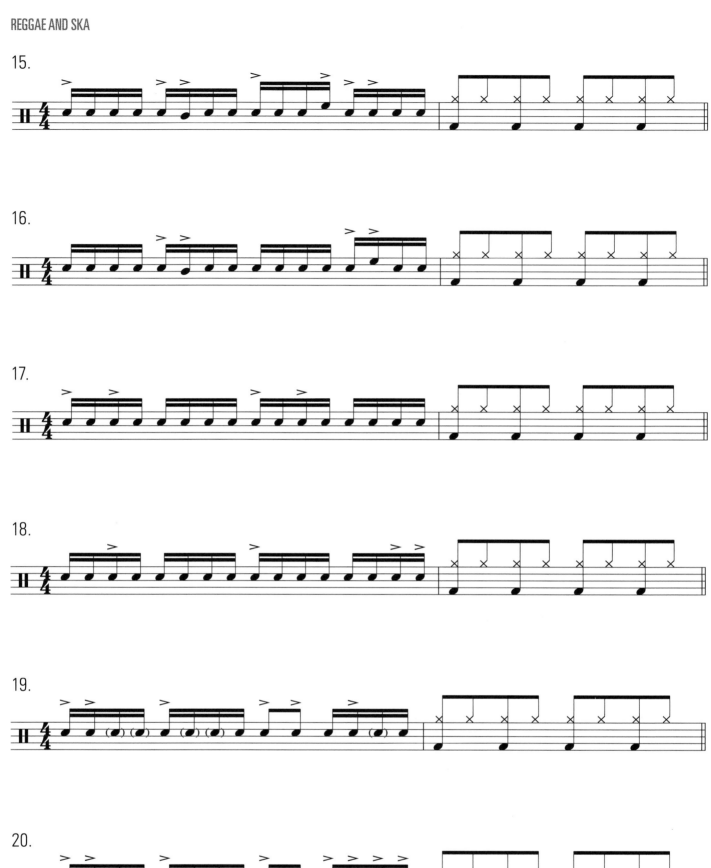

16.

17.

18.

19.

20.

21.

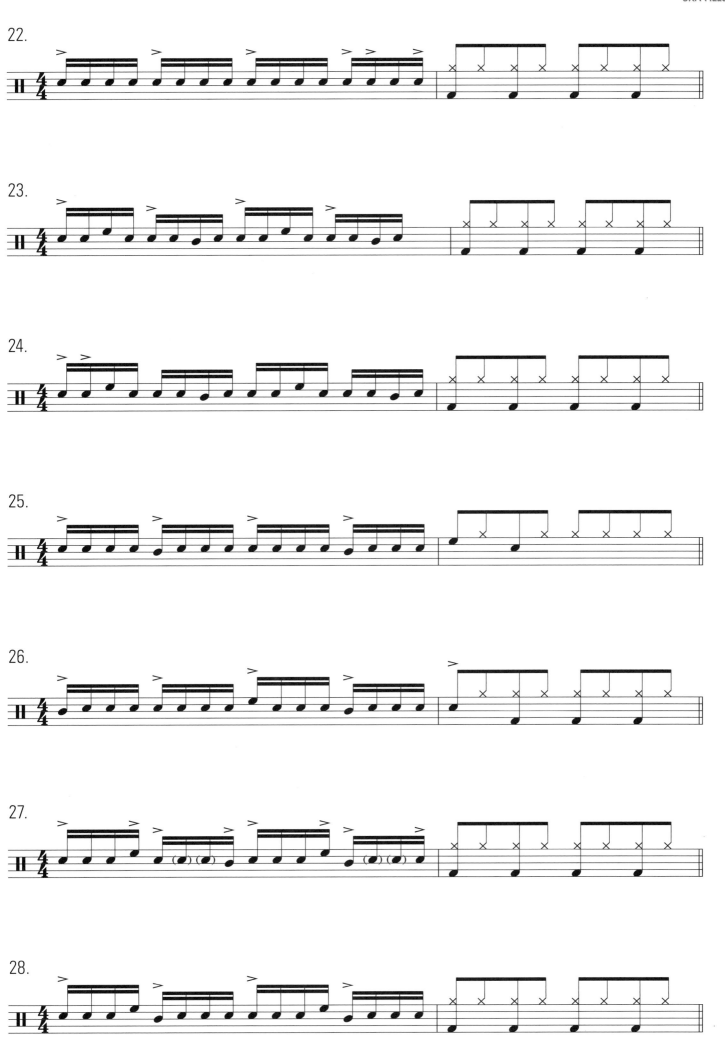

29.

30.

31.

32.

33.

34.

35.

ODD-TIME

6/8 FILLS

1.

2.

3.

4.

5.

6.

7.

8.

9.

10.

11.

12.

5/8 ROCK FILLS

1.

2.
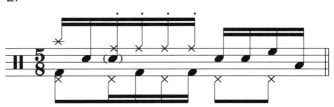

3.
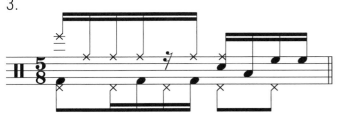

4.

5.

6.

7.

8.
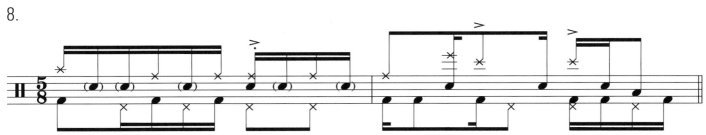

9.

10.
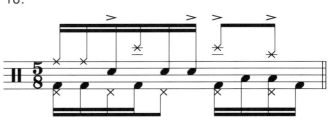

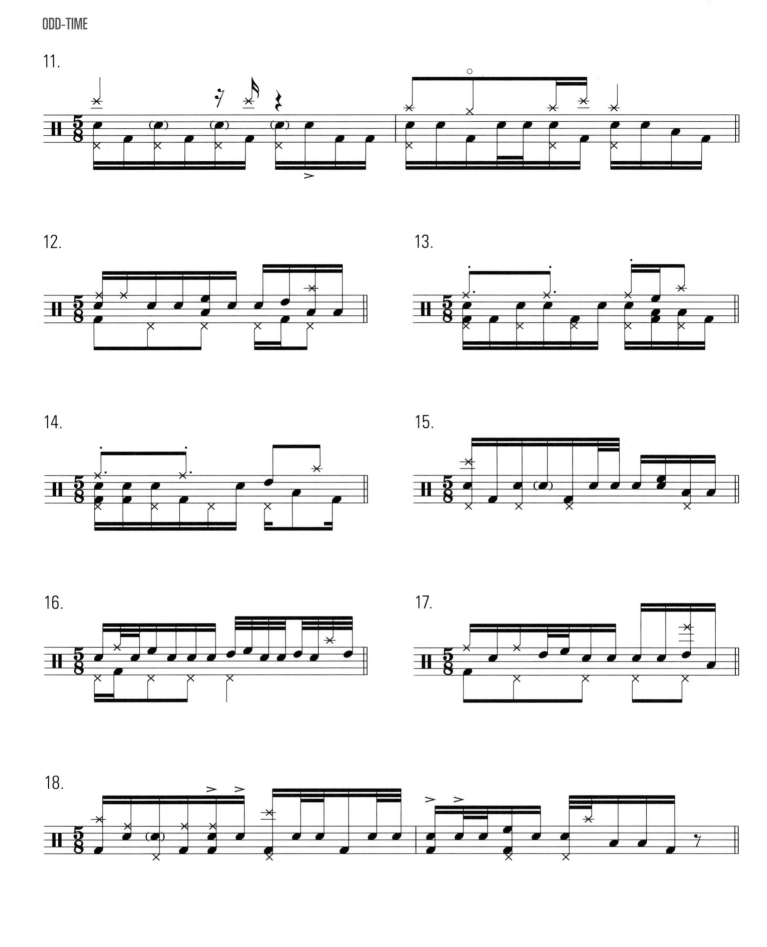

21.

22.

23.

24.

25.

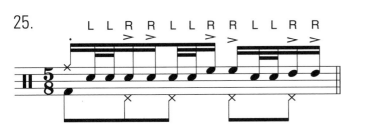

26.

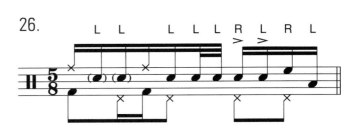

YOU CAN'T BEAT OUR DRUM BOOKS!

Learn to Play the Drumset – Book 1
by Peter Magadini

This unique method starts students out on the entire drumset and teaches them the basics in the shortest amount of time. Book 1 covers basic 4- and 5-piece set-ups, grips and sticks, reading and improvisation, coordination of hands and feet, and features a variety of contemporary and basic rhythm patterns with exercise breakdowns for each.

06620030 Book/CD Pack.. $14.99

Creative Timekeeping For The Contemporary Jazz Drummer
by Rick Mattingly

Combining a variety of jazz ride cymbal patterns with coordination and reading exercises, *Creative Timekeeping* develops true independence: the ability to play any rhythm on the ride cymbal while playing any rhythm on the snare and bass drums. It provides a variety of jazz ride cymbal patterns as well as coordination and reading exercises that can be played along with them. Five chapters: Ride Cymbal Patterns; Coordination Patterns and Reading; Combination Patterns and Reading; Applications; and Cymbal Reading.

06621764 .... $8.95

The Drumset Musician
by Rod Morgenstein and Rick Mattingly

Containing hundreds of practical, usable beats and fills, The Drumset Musician teaches you how to apply a variety of patterns and grooves to the actual performance of songs. The accompanying CD includes demos as well as 14 play-along tracks covering a wide range of rock, blues and pop styles, with detailed instructions on how to create exciting, solid drum parts.

06620011 Book/CD Pack.. $19.99

Drum Aerobics
by Andy Ziker

A 52-week, one-exercise-per-day workout program for developing, improving, and maintaining drum technique. Players of all levels – beginners to advanced – will increase their speed, coordination, dexterity and accuracy. The two CDs contain all 365 workout licks, plus play-along grooves in styles including rock, blues, jazz, heavy metal, reggae, funk, calypso, bossa nova, march, mambo, New Orleans 2nd Line, and lots more!

06620137 Book/2-CD Pack $19.99

40 Intermediate Snare Drum Solos
For Concert Performance
by Ben Hans

This book provides the advancing percussionist with interesting solo material in all musical styles. It is designed as a lesson supplement, or as performance material for recitals and solo competitions. Includes: 40 intermediate snare drum solos presented in easy-to-read notation; a music glossary; Percussive Arts Society rudiment chart; suggested sticking, dynamics and articulation markings; and much more!

06620067 .... $7.99

Joe Porcaro's Drumset Method – Groovin' with Rudiments
Patterns Applied to Rock, Jazz & Latin Drumset
by Joe Porcaro

Master teacher Joe Porcaro presents rudiments at the drumset in this sensational new edition of *Groovin' with Rudiments*. This book is chock full of exciting drum grooves, sticking patterns, fills, polyrhythmic adaptations, odd meters, and fantastic solo ideas in jazz, rock, and Latin feels. The enclosed CD features 99 audio clips examples in many styles to round out this true collection of superb drumming material for every serious drumset performer.

06620129 Book/CD Pack...$24.99

Show Drumming
The Essential Guide to Playing Drumset for Live Shows and Musicals
by Ed Shaughnessy and Clem DeRosa

Who better to teach you than "America's Premier Showdrummer" himself, Mr. Ed Shaughnessy! Features: a step-by-step walk-through of a simulated show; CD with music, comments & tips from Ed; notated examples; practical tips; advice on instruments; a special accessories section with photos; and more!

06620080 Book/CD Pack.. $16.95

Instant Guide to Drum Grooves
The Essential Reference for the Working Drummer
by Maria Martinez

Become a more versatile drumset player! From traditional Dixieland to cutting-edge hip-hop, Instant Guide to Drum Grooves is a handy source featuring 100 patterns that will prepare working drummers for the stylistic variety of modern gigs. The book includes essential beats and grooves in such styles as: jazz, shuffle, country, rock, funk, New Orleans, reggae, calypso, Brazilian and Latin.

06620056 Book/CD Pack.. $9.95

The Complete Drumset Rudiments
by Peter Magadini

Use your imagination to incorporate these rudimental etudes into new patterns that you can apply to the drumset or tom toms as you develop your hand technique with the Snare Drum Rudiments, your hand and foot technique with the Drumset Rudiments and your polyrhythmic technique with the Polyrhythm Rudiments. Adopt them all into your own creative expressions based on ideas you come up with while practicing.

06620016 Book/CD Pack.. $14.95

Drum Tuning
The Ultimate Guide
by Scott Schroedl

This book/CD pack is designed for drummers of all styles and levels. It contains step-by-step instruction along with over 35 professional photos that allow you to see the tools and tuning techniques up close. Covers: preparation; drumhead basics; drum construction and head properties; tom-toms; snare drum; bassdrum; the drum set as one instrument; drum sounds and tuning over the years; when to change heads; and more.

06620060 Book/CD Pack.. $14.95

FOR MORE INFORMATION, SEE YOUR LOCAL MUSIC DEALER, OR WRITE TO:

HAL•LEONARD®
CORPORATION

7777 W. BLUEMOUND RD. P.O. BOX 13819 MILWAUKEE, WI 53213

www.halleonard.com

Prices, contents, and availability subject to change without notice.

071